The
Seaside
Christmas Tree

Sarah Garland

The Seaside Christmas Tree

Stories and pictures by
Sarah Garland

Anna, Tom and Tilly went down
to the sea.

"Let's make a Christmas tree,"
said Anna.

They looked for presents for the
tree. Anna found a boot, Tom
found a bottle

and Tilly found a . . .

Anna found a box, Tom found
a rope

and Tilly found a . . .

Anna found a pipe, Tom found
a net

and Tilly found a . . .

23

Tilly played Father Christmas.

29